BROKEN RECORDS

ANIMAL RECORDS

TO DIG YOUR CLAWS INTO!

KENNY ABDO

Fly!
An Imprint of Abdo Zoom
abdobooks.com

abdobooks.com

Published by Abdo Zoom, a division of ABDO, P.O. Box 398166, Minneapolis, Minnesota 55439.

Printed in the United States of America, North Mankato, Minnesota.
052023
092023

THIS BOOK CONTAINS RECYCLED MATERIALS

Photo Credits: AP Images, Getty Images, Newscom, Shutterstock, ©Cherie Molloy pCover, 14, 15, ©Tammy Ven Dange p12
Production Contributors: Kenny Abdo, Jennie Forsberg, Grace Hansen
Design Contributors: Candice Keimig, Neil Klinepier, Laura Graphenteen

Library of Congress Control Number: 2022946916

Publisher's Cataloging-in-Publication Data

Names: Abdo, Kenny, author.
Title: Animal records to dig your claws into! / by Kenny Abdo
Description: Minneapolis, Minnesota : Abdo Zoom, 2024 | Series: Broken records | Includes online resources and index.
Identifiers: ISBN 9781098281373 (lib. bdg.) | ISBN 9781098282073 (ebook) | ISBN 9781098282424 (Read-to-me ebook)
Subjects: LCSH: Records--Juvenile literature. | History--Juvenile literature. | Animals--Juvenile literature.
Classification: DDC 032.02--dc23

TABLE OF CONTENTS

ANIMAL RECORDS

Records broken by humans have thrilled people throughout history. So, when our furry and feathery friends reach for greatness, their records come with a lot of bite!

19

From skateboarding pups to feline **social media influencers**, amazing animal records have clawed their way into history!

BROKEN RECORDS

average 3 lb ostrich egg

An egg weighing almost 6 lbs (2.72 kg) was laid by an **ostrich** in 2008. It became the largest egg from a living bird, making a record that is all it is cracked up to be!

Otto the bulldog is a good boy for more than one reason. In 2015, he skateboarded through the legs of 30 people. Otto set the record for the longest human tunnel travelled through by a skateboarding dog!

In 2015, Chris, an Australian **ram**, was named the world´s woolliest sheep. Chris had more than 88 lbs (40 kg) of **wool** shaved from him! A lot of sweaters could be made from that!

In 2020, golden retriever Finley Molloy wowed the world! By holding six tennis balls in his mouth at one time, Finley claimed the **Guinness World Record**!

In 2022, the world wished Jonathan the **tortoise** a happy 190th birthday!

Guinness gifted him the record for world's oldest tortoise ever!

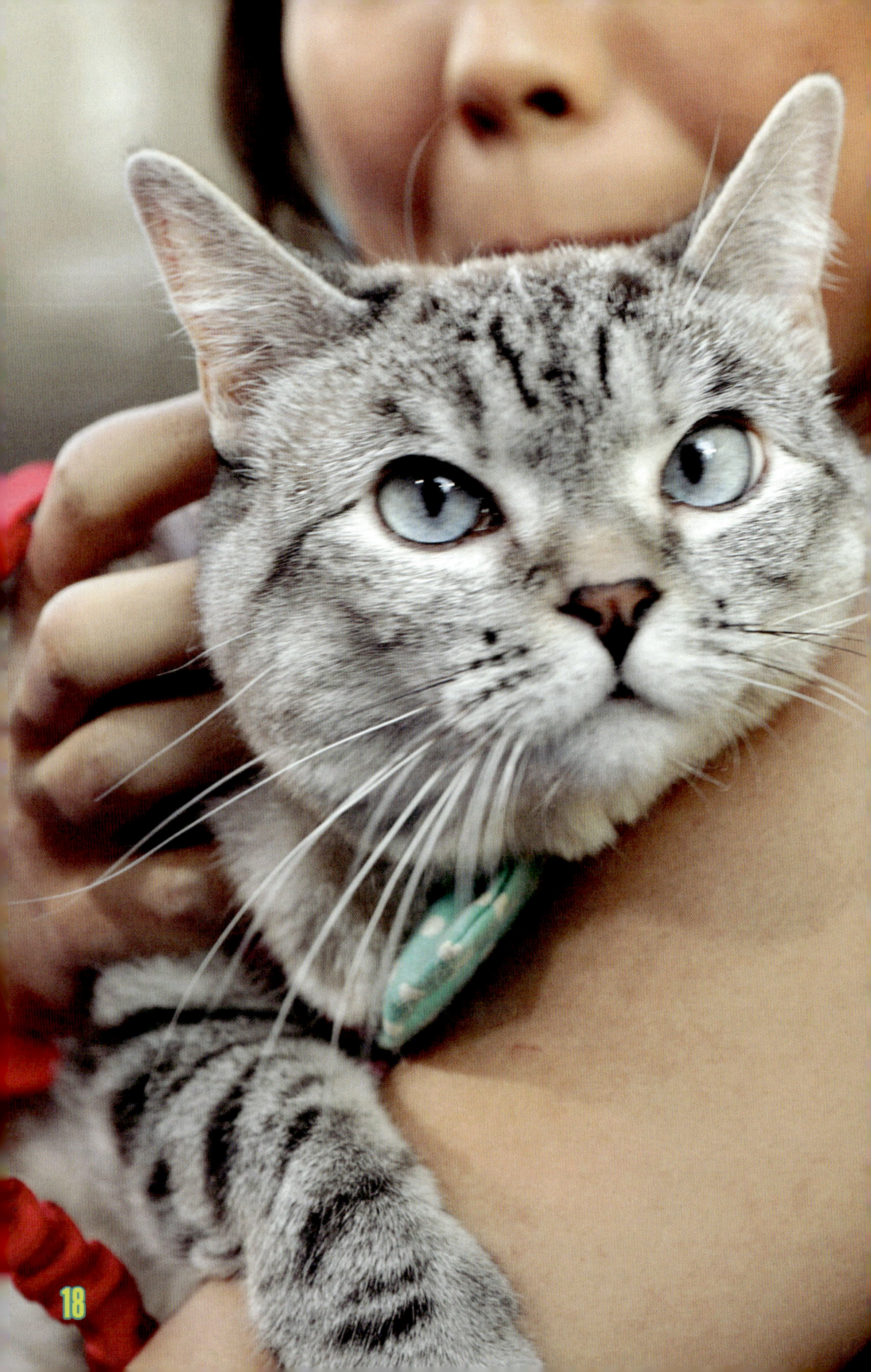

In a world full of **influencers**, none are nearly as pur-fect as Nala the cat. As of 2023, the Siamese-tabby has 4.4 million Instagram followers. It is the record for most followers on the **social media** platform for a cat.

FOR THE RECORD

With so many records to be broken, the animals that take on the nearly impossible aren't *kitten* around!

GLOSSARY

Guinness World Record – an award given to those who have broken a record never achieved before.

influencer – or a social media influencer, is an influential person in social media networks, often with a large following, who promotes products and services of a brand.

ostrich – a large, powerful African bird that can run very fast but cannot fly.

ram – a male sheep.

social media – websites and apps that allow users to create and share content or participate in social networking.

tortoise – a turtle that lives on land.

wool – a natural hair-like fiber produced year-round by various animals, including sheep.

ONLINE RESOURCES

Booklinks
NONFICTION NETWORK
FREE! ONLINE NONFICTION RESOURCES

To learn more about animal records, please visit **abdobooklinks.com** or scan this QR code. These links are routinely monitored and updated to provide the most current information available.

INDEX